Danielle Steel:
50 Love and Life Lessons
from Reading Danielle Steel
Romance Novels

Cleopatra Mark

ISBN:1535447052
ISBN-13:9781535447058

DEDICATION

This book is dedicated to all the women around the world reading romance novels. We are women struggling to grapple with the complexities of life. We are women who appreciate all the forms that love will come to us. We know how important love is from womb to tomb.

CONTENTS

ACKNOWLEDGMENTS

I want to acknowledge my best friends who all love Danielle Steel. We read the same books together so that we can talk about them over glasses of red wine. They are all working women who asked that I leave their last names out of the book. I understand. Romance novels are something only women understand or at least that is what we have decided. These best friends are Jayna C, Tracy B., Pam M., Deb M, Preston S., Ann E., Cynthia L., and Patricia H. Okay, Ernie and Dan are part of this group too. They are two gay men who have been together for 40 years. They love a good romance novel and a glass of red wine, too.

AUTHOR NAME

1 INTRODUCTION TO DANIELLE STEEL

Danielle Fernandes Dominique, popularly known as Danielle Steel is a prolific American novelist who has sold more than 800 million copies to earn the title of the best selling living author and the fourth bestselling writer of all times. The czarina of romantic fiction is based in California and has had her books translated into a staggering 28 languages with 22 of them being adapted into television series. A couple of them have even received the prestigious Golden Globe nominations. Steel is known for her ability to write multiple books simultaneously, sometimes even five at a time.

She sticks to a standard formula that has worked wonders for her, and won her rave reviews along with a rather loyal readership, spanning across continents. Danielle Steel's plots almost always revolve around rich families living in opulent estates, who later go on to face crisis that threaten their position in society. As the novel unfolds, they are besieged by dark and twisted elements such as fraud, conviction, blackmail, extra marital affairs, suicide and the likes.

While she has also published children's books and poetry, Steel is primarily known for her romance and family based paperbacks.

THE EARLY YEARS

Born to John Schulein-Steel (a German-Jewish immigrant) and Norma da Camara Stone dos Reis (the Portugal born child of a diplomat), Danielle Steel was raised as a Catholic, and has expressed a desire to be a nun during her growing up years. Much of her life was spent in France where she got an up, close and personal opportunity to view the high life that is so emblematic of her novels. He observed the habits, mannerisms and attitudes of the rich and famous and deftly incorporated them into her penchant for story-telling.

Her parents ended their marriage when she was eight, and this brought Steel to New York City where she was primarily raised by her father, with little opportunity to interact with her mother. Steel also accompanied her father on several trips to Europe. This explains how quickly she took to the European way of life, and how several of her popular novels including Jewels, features a prominent European backdrop.

Steel began writing short stories as a child, and while in her teens she was already dabbling in poetry. A graduate from the Lycee Francis de New York in 1963, Danielle studied fashion design and literature design, initially from the Parsons School of Design and subsequently from the New York University.

STARTING AS A WRITER

At 18, Danielle Steel went on to marry French-American banking professional Claude-Eric Lazard. As a teenage wife, she was attending New York University, and simultaneously worked on her first manuscript the subsequent year. She was employed with a New York public relations agency for a long while after the birth of her daughter in 1966. It was an impressed magazine client who encouraged her to concentrate on her writing skills, and urged her to draft a book, which she went on to do. Later, Steel moved to San Francisco, where she briefly worked in the copywriting department of Grey Advertising.

PERSONAL LIFE THAT INSPIRED HER NOVELS

After nine tumultuous years, fraught with extended periods of separation, Steel and Lazard finally divorced. Going Home, her first novel released in 1972, and was symbolic of the most predominant themes of all the books that followed it. It focused on a genre that Steel came to be known for, that defined her writing style and became her unique selling point. It emphasized on issues related to relationships, marriages and families.

Much of the characteristic drama that dominated the plot of her novels, including her first published book, was inspired by the events in her personal life.

While still being the wife of Lazard, Steel got introduced to Dany Zugelder, when she was interviewing a prison inmate near Lompoc, California. Zegelder was an inmate in the same premises. During his parole in 1973, he lived with Steel, but had to return to prison on rape and theft charges in 1974. In 1975, Steel married Zugelder dramatically in the jail canteen after her divorce with Lazard came through. Though they divorced in 1978, the relationship inspired her next couple of novels – Passion's Promise and Now and Forever, which launched her eventful career as a novelist.

Steel went on to get hitched with her third husband a day after her divorce with Zugelder came through. William George Goth and Danille Steel stayed married until 1981, during which she gave birth to a son. With her fourth novel, Promise, she became a regular in San Francisco's high society circles, while Goth remained in the shadows of drug addiction.

In 1981, Steel tied the knot for the fourth time with John Triana. They went on to have five children, Samantha, Victoria, Vanessa, Maxx and Zara.

BREAKING ALL RECORDS

Steel has been a consistent fixture on the New York Times bestseller list for both hardcovers and paperbacks since her marriage to John Triana. In fact, in 1989 she made her way into the Guinness Book of World Records for having her books featured on the New York Times Bestseller List for the maximum number of consecutive years for any author- 381 to be precise. Since her foray into the world of writing, each of the novels penned by her has been a bestseller. In 1984, Steel drafted her first non-fictional work titled, Having a Baby, which chronicled her own misadventures with miscarriage.

Danielle Steel was so committed to spending more time with her children that she often wrote at night, sleeping only for a few hours. She developed a rather dexterous method of working on several titles simultaneously. While one book was being edited, she was writing a book and outlining another. The prolific writer was sometimes rumored to be working on five book projects at a time.

Steel courted matrimony for the fifth time with finance professional Thomas James Perkins, only to divorce in 2002. Her book The Klone and I is said to be a result of a personal joke with Perkins. In 2006, Perkin's wrote the book Sex and the Single Zillionaire and dedicated it to Danielle Steel.

In 2002, Steel was conferred with the title of an Officer of the Ordre Des Arts et des Lettres by the French government for contributing significantly to world culture.

She has been conferred with several awards such as Distinguished Service in Mental Health Award from the New York Presbyterian Hospital, Columbia University Medical School and Cornell Medical College. She also received the Outstanding Achievement Award for working with adolescents from Larkin Street Youth Services in San Francisco, along with the Distinguished Service Award from the American Psychiatric Association.

In 2006, Danielle Steel tied up with Elizabeth Arden to launch, Danielle by Danielle Steel, her signature fragrance.

HOME AND ARTS

After years of incessant writing, Danielle launched a San Francisco art gallery that showcased modern works of art and exhibited paintings and artifacts of upcoming artists. Though the gallery shut in 2007, Steel still curates shows at the Andre Schwartz Gallery in San Francisco.

Steel now shuttles between her residence in San Francisco (the erstwhile 1913 mansion of Adolph Spreckels, a sugar businessman) and a second villa in Paris. Irrespective of her very public profile and diverse undertakings, the lady remains discreet and elusive. She is not known to court tabloid headlines/interviews and feverishly protects her kids from the media. Danielle Steel is rarely known to make public appearances or consent to interviews.

HER WRITINGS

Danielle Steel's novels are read in 47 nations all over the world after being translated into 28 languages. Often referred to formulaic, the plot in her books tend to revolve around a family crisis that shakes the foundations of relationships. While detractors have slammed her for creating unrealistic characters and unreal settings of the rich and famous, Steel has a compelling grip over human emotions and relationships. She deals with concerns such as death, family crisis, illness, separation and loss, with a deep understanding and sensitivity. There are rumors about many events in her novels being inspired by her life, comprising multiple marriages, con husbands and other details that were kept hidden from her public profile.

Though she has been accused time and again of resorting to fluff, Steel touches the unpleasant aspects of human behavior such as suicide, war, incest and separation with ease. Her writings grew with time. From docile and submissive, her female protagonists grew more assertive and authoritative in later novels. They began to seek the life of their choice if they find it with their current partner.

She also began taking greater risks with the story-line in her recent works. For instance, Ransom is more of a suspense thriller than her staple romance genre, tracking the lives of three sets of characters as their destiny entwines. Toxic

Bachelors, on the other hand, is a stark deviation from her standard style in the sense that it's a story told through the perspective of three commitment phobic men who finally discover their real loves.

Another thing that Steel is often criticized for is her extremely redundant and elaborate, often bordering on verbose, story-telling. She tells the story very explicitly rather than pointing it out to readers to help them experience and interpret it according to their imagination. This can sometimes gives the illusion of looking from the outside rather than actually being a part of the story. Danielle Steel refrains from wiring sequels to avoid any comparisons with her earlier works.

ADAPTATIONS

About twenty-two of Danielle Steel's books have been converted into television series, with a couple of them (Jewels was one of them) receiving Golden Globe nominations. Jewels, a novel about the survival of a female protagonist and children in a war torn setting during World War II, and their subsequent rise as one of Europe's largest jewelry houses. The first movie studio that offered to buy the rights of Danielle Steel's The Ghost was Columbia Pictures. She also tied up with New Line Home Entertainment to purchase the movie rights to 30 books authored by her for DVD showcasing.

THE NICHOLAS TRAINA CONTROVERSY

In 1993 Danielle Steel sued a writer who set out to reveal in her book that Steel's son Nick was in fact adopted by her then husband John Triana though adoption records in California are sealed. The judge pronounced an exceptionally unusual ruling letting Nick's adoption seal to overturn, though he was a minor. The order was upheld by the California Appellate Judge, who pronounced that since Steel was well-known, the adoption of her son did not come with similar privacy rights as others. The book was ultimately awarded the right to be published.

Nicholas Traina, a member of San Francisco's bands Link 80 and Knowledge, committed suicide in 1997. Steel penned her Bright Lights in Nick's memory, the proceeds for which were channeled to fund establishments working for the treatment of mental illness. Steel has lobbied determinedly in Washington for legislation related to gaining widespread awareness of mental illnesses in children. She also held fund raisers bi-annually in San Francisco, referred to as The Star Ball.

DOESN'T CONSIDER HERSELF A ROMANCE NOVELIST

In 2012 Danielle Steel raised plenty of eyebrows when she declared on a CBS early morning show that she didn't consider herself a romance writer. Some were of the view that she was slamming a genre made so popular by her. But by and large, her statement does ring true if viewed in the right perspective. She is by and large a relationships writer who focuses on a multitude of familial relationships within a romantic or challenge ridden story-line. It wouldn't do her justice to say her books are only about romance, though romance does play a significant part in many plots.

Steel offers a glamorous and glitzy preview into the lives of the wealthy and famous. The settings range from World War II to Hollywood to showcase the lives of intriguing characters whose near perfect lives have been threatened due to certain plot twisting dark occurrences in their lives. This leads to a journey of self-discovery as they realize that life gives them another chance once they are strong enough to rise above their circumstances.

If anything Danielle Steel can be safely referred to as women's fiction author which isn't the same as a romance author, since women's fiction comprise a multitude of writing styles that do not necessarily fit into the genre of romantic fiction. Her endings are not always the picture perfect endings craved for by romance novel addicts. They tend to be more mature, realistic and bittersweet. Just like real life, there are no guaranteed happy endings in her books.

Danielle Steel: 50 Lessons of Love and Life from her Readers

2 DANIELLE STEEL'S MOST ICONIC WORKS

While Steel wrote prolifically, sometimes juggling even five books at a time to meet her publisher's and readers' demands, some of her most iconic books are Heartbeat, Jewels, The Promise, The Gift, Big Girl, No Greater Love, A Perfect Stranger, Betrayal, Accident, The Wedding, Family Ties, Changes, Malice, Sisters, Kaleidoscope and more.

Heartbeat is about Bill Thigpen, an ace scriptwriter and producer for television's most popular daytime soap, who is soaring in his career while his marriage is collapsing. Cut to nine years ahead, he is living a solitary life in Hollywood and still relishing the sweet smell of success. His life is near perfect with expensive vacations, causal flings and chartbuster ratings.

Adrian Townsend believed she has everything she ever wanted (a successful career as a TV production assistant) and was living the perfect American Dream with her husband (an upcoming professional in his industry). The twist in the tale comes once she gets pregnant, and is asked by the husband to choose between him and the baby.

Bill and Adrian bump into each other at a supermarket. Looking at her, he suddenly yearns for more. To be with a woman he truly loves and to live a fulfilled family life. He is not prepared to deal with complications of another man's child and a new wife. They both didn't want it but both couldn't help being drawn to one another. The author attempts to touch the Heartbeat of two people as they forge their initial friendship into love, while meeting the obstacles in their life with courage and humor.

Heartbeat is highly symbolic of the formulaic plots and writing style of Danielle Steel. It is about people who live the good life but are stuck when it comes to personal relationships. They often go about seeking the love they haven't found in their existing relationships. And though there is an initial resistance, the characters can't help but be drawn to each other in their shared experiences of incompleteness and quest for true love.

Jewels is a signature Danielle Steel family masterpiece that revolves around the life of Sarah Whitfield whose seventy-fifth birthday brings back several memories of her broken marriage, and a subsequent trip to Europe where she meets William, the Duke of Whitfield. William doesn't think twice before giving up his right to the throne to have Sarah as his dutchess and wife. The war begins just after their honeymoon when they purchase a grand erstwhile French chateau. William joins the forces, while Sarah is left to tend to their infant and an unborn child. The chateau is taken over by the Nazis, forcing Sarah to lead a life of deprivation and fear, while still believing her husband is alive.

Post war, the Whitfields take to purchasing jewels sold by broke war survivors. Sarah's sense of style and a keen eye for beauty allows her to bag an enviable collection of prestigious pieces. Soon, Whitfield's jewelry store is launched in Paris. The business grows fast, and more stores make their way into London and Rome. This classic Danielle Steel family saga has all the elements of war, intrigue, love, family strength and more. At its crux were the various characters and their relationships with one another. The firstborn Phillip is proud and obstinate, while the second son Julian is generous, warm hearted and amiable. Isabella is headstrong and rebellious, while Xavier is wild and unique.

With backdrops chronicling challenging world events and wars, Danielle Steel often reinforced the strength of family in conquering seemingly insurmountable situations. She emphasized that though families are not perfect and that our relationship with your family members may be far from perfect, there's nothing quite as powerful a force in meeting life's challenges as family.

Big Girl was a path-breaking novel for Danielle Steel since she deviated from her norms of perfect beauty. From gorgeous looking protagonists with fine cheekbones, blue eyes and a sultry frame she went to a chubby protagonist with average looks. The book was about unconventional beauty, discovering oneself and learning to accept ourselves, with all the flaws.

Victoria is often referred to as "our tester cake" by her father for her ordinary looks, while her younger sister Gracie is the epitome of perfect beauty. Jim, Victoria's father and Christina, her mother (both conventionally good-looking) are relieved at getting it right with Gracie. Victoria lands her dream job of a teacher but is never successful at getting her parent's acceptance. Despite all the awkwardness, she is close to her sibling, and they reveal nothing but unconditional love for each other. However, Victoria has to forever contend with her parent's displeasure.

The plot takes a compelling turn when Grace gets engaged to a person whose persona is much like her own father.

Victoria is concerned about her sister's happiness, but feels like an utter failure without a man. The wedding brings with it a serendipitous encounter, an act of choking betrayal and a huge confrontation within the family leading to a plot twist. Big Girl is all about Victoria's quest to believe in herself, celebrate herself and be proud of the victories she has battled hard for.

3
25 POWERFUL LOVE AND LIFE LESSONS TO ABSORB FROM DANIELLE STEEL'S ROMANCE BOOKS

1. Love Always Deserves Another Chance

Several of Danielle Steel's books focus on giving love a second chance. When love is not perfect, Steel's characters, despite the initial resistance, go out there and surrender themselves to love and forgiving themselves again. From Heartbeat's Adrian to Bittersweet's India, they are all prepared to walk down the tricky yet fulfilling path of friendship, real love and romance all over again.

Danielle Steel's characters though lost and disillusioned with love at some point do not hesitate in giving it another chance when they recognize the power of true love. They don't shy away from falling in love again and again until they experience the love they deserve. Though sometimes the characters hesitate in giving love another chance due to unfortunate incidents related to previous relationships, they still allow themselves the vulnerability of opening themselves up to love once again.

2. Nothing Can Keep You Apart If You're Destined To Be With Your Loved One

Irrespective of the circumstances, challenges and forces that pull you apart temporarily, nothing can keep two souls far away if they are destined to be together. Michael and Nancy, protagonists from The Promise illustrate this poignant lesson of love beautifully. When love is meant to be, it will be. When two karmically connected souls are meant to be together, the universe will find a means to bring them together.

3. Love Can Be Found in the Midst of the Greatest Tragedies

A lot of Steel's books have been set in the backdrop of tumultuous situations such as war, natural catastrophes and The Holocaust. However, despite the rough circumstances around them, Steel's protagonists sometimes manage to find a silver lining in the form of love, leading to the belief that love can be found in the most challenging and unlikeliest circumstances.

4. Love Can Heal You

Like Grace, the protagonist from Steel's blockbuster, Malice, there may be a dark past filled with unpleasant secrets haunting you for life. However, there's a little hope and love can change it all. Grace encounters a New York lawyer after experiencing a series of brutal crimes, horrible secrets and spending a lifetime as a victim, paying for other's sins.

However a chance at love gives her hope, the power to heal herself and the opportunity of a perfect life she hadn't even dreamt about earlier. Love gives you the strength and insight to triumph over all evil forces in your life and to transform a life filled with pain into being a blessing for those around you.

5. Love at First Sight is Indeed Possible

Can you fall in love with someone you've only just seen? Is it possible to feel a deep connection with someone you haven't even spoken to yet? If Steel's romance novels are be believed, a thumping yes! From Bill and Adrian of Heartbeat to Raphaella and Alexander from A Perfect Stranger, it is all about feeling an instant connection. It makes you believe that despite rationalists stating otherwise, love at first sight can be possible. Irrespective of our differences and diversities, we can fall in love with a person with whom we experience an immediate karmic connection.

6. When the Time's Right, Things Will Fall in Place

In a few of her novels including the popular Wanderlust, Charlie leaves Audrey in messy war ridden circumstances.

Later, Audrey explains   why she didn't marry him and he doesn't think much about waiting for her. Charlie gets married to another girl even though Audrey loves him deeply.

Later, Charlie separates from his wife and gets back to Audrey. Audrey, being very much in love with him, accepts him back in her life with open arms. It just shows when the time for a relationship is right, it will happen, no matter what. What we often believe to be the end of a relationship may simply not be the right time for the relationship.

We may love a person and lose him/her due to circumstances, choices, ill-fated decisions etc. but when the time is right, nothing can stop the love from coming back to us.

7. We Don't Really Have Much Time

Danielle Steel deals with tragedies such as death, illnesses, suicide etc. with sensitivity and deftness. Her protagonists are always going through a life-changing situation that offers them a whole new perspective of life.

For instance, Bernie from Fine Things is coming to terms with his perfect family life crumbling like a pack of cards after his wife Liz is diagnosed with cancer. He prepares himself to face the loss bravely and humorously for the sake of his two young kids. Bernie learns precious life lessons in the process. The biggest being that while we are busy chasing our dreams, we forget to stop and think that we really don't have much time with our loved ones.

8. Opposites Attract

Many of Danielle Steel's protagonists come from starkly different backgrounds, have conflicting views, diverse personas – in other words – even though her characters come from different worlds they still find themselves being drawn to each other through an immediate and irresistible attractions.

Take law school dropout Coco Barrington and dashing British actor Leslie Baxter from One Day at a Time. They couldn't be any more different. Coco is the proverbial black sheep in a family of stalwarts, while Leslie has the world swooning over his good looks and effortless charm.

Conventionally, no one would have imagined such diagrammatically different personas to feel an overpowering attraction for each other. But Danielle Steel's intriguing writing makes us realize that it is possible to love people who are different from us. It also makes us see things from a whole new perspective of the other person, which we may never have seen otherwise.

9. You Need To Keep an Open Mind

Even when things have gone awry with previous relationships, it isn't the end of the love road for you. You must keep an open heart and mind and give yourself the strength to love again. It may not be easy, but nothing in life that is worth having is ever easy. You may be carrying the burden, pain, destruction and loss of the past, but that doesn't mean you don't give a fulfilling future an honest chance. Everybody deserves love

In Danielle Steel's Safe Harbor, Matt and Ophelia are both dealing with their own losses when they are brought together by the forces of destiny to give themselves a chance at true love again. Though it seems near impossible at first, given the circumstances they've been through in their lives, an eternal connection and shared grief doesn't fail to bring their hearts together. They find themselves being irrevocably drawn to each other in their quest for a fulfilling relationship. Both gradually open themselves up to the shared joys and sorrows of love. With patience, dedication and faith, they find themselves on the brink of happily ever after yet again.

10. We Will Pull Through No Matter What the Situation

Danielle Steel's novels are full of happy people facing unexpected tragedies that throw their life on the path of devastation. There's everything from war to widowhood to suicide to losing your loved ones to terminal illnesses.

However, the one thing that stands out in the accomplished author's novels is that her characters never give up. No matter what the situation, they always rise above it and take life head on to emerge even more victorious than before. They convert unfortunate events into opportunities to transform into stronger and better people. There's no wallowing in self-pity forever. For the sake of their loved ones, the protagonists just get up, brush aside all the dust and learn to live and love again.

In Zoya, the protagonist Zoya has to face innumerable challenges in the backdrop of the Russian Revolution and the Depression. Her life is a whirlwind of losses, disasters and fighting tragedies. Yet, she never gives up and goes about rebuilding her life with strength and courage. Danielle Steel often tells stories of rare, courageous and spirited women who refuse to give up even in the face of unimaginable tragedies.

This is also true for Sarah Whitfield from Jewels. She experiences war, loss, terror, deprivation and several other challenging conditions, only to emerge a survivor who not just does a wonderful job of bringing up her children but also plays an instrumental role in creating a jewelry store empire all over Europe. Her fine eye for beauty, grit, determination and goodness help her conquer the tragedies in her life, and even turn them into opportunities. She epitomized the belief that you are bigger than any situation that you think can shake you up. Your determination, strength and undying spirit is what will help you sail through tough times.

11. You're Never Too Old to Find True Love

Danielle Steel's books scoff at those who believe true love cannot be experienced after a certain age. Her protagonists are not giddy-headed teens, rather successful, mature and self-assured women who recognize the power of true love when it happens. They know life has given them another chance and they cherish it.

Melanie Adams from Changes has two teenage daughters and has been through a tumultuous marriage and relationship. Her age or experiences, however don't stop her from feeling the power of true love when it she encounters Peter Hallam, a widower and successful surgeon, with three children. Though both are far from young romantics, they open themselves up for love.

Danielle Steel's novels always emphasize that there's really no age to fall in love and that true love will come into you when the time is right.

12. Family is the Strongest Bond of All

Danielle Steel crafts magnificent stories around the institution of family. Her novels are dripping with tales about how despite all the challenges and changing equations within the family, it is the single largest bond that helps us tide through difficult phases. There may be plenty of differences, dark secrets, tragedies, raw emotions and changing relationships, but one thing's that's the center of it all is blood is thicker than water and at the end of the day, it's only your family that you can fall back on. Family has the power to accept you and love you unconditionally. It will help you tide through any situation with love, acceptance and care.

Take Steel's protagonist Annie Ferguson from Family Ties for instance. She is just on a the brink of starting her life with a career and boyfriend, when tragedy strikes and her life is thrown off the balance when she has to be a single mother to her sister's three orphaned kids. She puts her entire life on hold for devotedly bringing up the children to keep a promise she made. As the story progresses, the now young adults present her with a new set of parenting challenges.

Annie experiences everything from the empty nest syndrome to dealing with rebellious young adults. There's also a sudden encounter that's destined to alter her life forever. With all the challenges she tackles, one thing reigns supreme – family bonds are indeed the strongest ones we ever experience in our lifetime. They hold us, keep us grounded yet allow us to soar.

Family bonds are also beautifully articulated in Steel's, The Wedding. At the heart of Alegra's (the daughter of respected Hollywood couple Simon Steinberg and Blaire Scott) wedding preparations is the tale of different generations from the Stenberg family struggling with broken promises and new chances. The book talks about bridging the gap between past events and future hopes. It is about reconciliations and forgiveness.

Family Album is another signature Danielle Steel masterpiece that talks about the powerful force of family bonds. It's the story of Faye Price, a legendary Hollywood actress who fulfills her dream of being the industry's pioneer woman directors. However, despite her roaring success, the one thing she holds on to preciously is her family of five children.

They are constantly challenged in a world faced with changing family dynamics to finally face one of the harshest tests families can be subjected to. This helps them come out even stronger as a family that is forever tied with love, faith and undying loyalty.

13. Everyone Walks in and Out of Your Life for a Reason

Danielle Steel's books brilliantly portray the idea that every person who walks into your life is there for a reason. It is to contribute to who you are as a person.

Even people who walk out of your life move out for a reason and not without teaching you some of life's most important lessons. The one's who cease to be a part of your life also give you several untold gifts by simply being a part of your life for a brief period of time. They make you wise and strong, and equip you to deal with all future relationships with maturity, compassion and understanding. There is an undeniable role that every person plays in your life, and this is poignantly reinforced in Steel's The Gift.

The Gift talks about a young lady who gets out of a Chicago bound bus to a tiny Midwestern town. The lady isn't there to stay. She's just a passerby who stops there for a reason, which forms the crux of the story. Even though people are not meant to be a part of our lives forever, they will play their part and move on to teach us the greatest lessons of life.

14. We Must Learn To Love Ourselves Before Anybody Else Does

Danielle Steel deftly drives across the message of being able to love and accept ourselves before we expect someone else to love us. Through stories like Big Girl, there is an emphasis on being able to celebrate your strengths and weaknesses and discovering yourself to love yourself unconditionally.

Big Girl tells the story of Victoria, who is the average looking older daughter of a good-looking and distinguished couple. Victoria's sister Grace is as flawless looking as her parents, who admit to getting it right with Grace and chide Victoria as being their less than impressive tester cake. Grace gets engaged and Victoria is left feeling like a failure all over again.

She's coming to terms with a lifetime of not being up to the mark, hurt, neglect and pain that she's subjected to by her disapproving parents. However, she comes to terms with the challenge of accepting herself, and celebrating her pluses and minuses to finally stake her claim to life's victories she's passionately fought for. Victoria discovers irrespective of her size and looks, she is terrific.

15. Abused Bodies and Spirits Heal Eventually

Danielle Steel deals with issues related to domestic abuse and child abuse with the sensitivity of a pro. Rather than painting rosy, candy-floss pictures of a perfect world, she doesn't hesitate to explore the darker sides of human existence. The issues that are often not talked about and buried under the carpet of pretentious images and seemingly perfect lives.

In The Long Road Home Garbriella and Joe are both facing the ghosts of their abusive childhoods, and struggle to survive and come to terms with their tumultuous past. Eventually, Gabriella works towards healing her broken world, and is able to shake off the guilt of abuse to discover forgiveness.

The story vividly portrays the challenges faced by victims of abuse and how they embark on a gradual process of healing that leads to ultimate forgiveness. It talks about gathering yourself, loving yourself and getting rid of all the guilt.

Even in Journey, Maddy's healing commences when she becomes a part of the First Lady's Commission on Violence Against Women. There she learns about familiar yet harsh stories of terror-struck girlfriends and wives, while also meeting an eminent diplomat, Bill Alexander. He manages to open her eyes to reality and accept that she's in a terribly wrong marriage. Thus begins a journey of healing from the pain of an abusive marriage by finding strength from within.

Another Danielle Steel ace, Malice, has Grace Adams

healing her pain by reaching out to other abused children and womenfolk that live a nightmarish life she's much too familiar with. She meets Charles Mackenzie, a hotshot New York lawyer who wants to give the perfect life she's always dreamt of. He wants Grace to be healed and to raise a family with him. Grace is however vulnerable to an enemy from the past that continues to haunt her and threaten her quest for happiness.

16. Friendships Are Forever

Danielle Steel's novels inspire deep bonds of friendships. They talk about friends that face challenges, find strength in each other, take life's adventures head on, and endure everything from loss, dark realities and trials through an unforgettable journey of togetherness. They are about life's most vital bonds that are forged by choice and by opening your hearts to strangers.

Friends Forever traces the life of five kids who meet in kindergarten. They go on to become thick friends for life. The story tracks their journey with all its trials and tribulations as they form bonds of a lifetime. As Gabby, Izzie, Sean, Billy and Andy go from grade school to their teen years, their lives are littered with families that are coming apart, unfortunate decisions and losses. They take recourse into their gang of five to deal with the storms in their life. However, as life progresses, the storms get riskier and the losses much sharper. The right road seems harder to pick in a journey comprising love, friendship and survival.

Steel's The Ranch also explores the complexities and hidden facets of lifelong friendships beautifully. It talks about three college friends, who had been really thick in their teens, move on in different directions as life progresses. They go on to achieve a different status and position in life, while facing a multitude of challenges and secrets. However, one thing at the core of their life that remains steady is their friendship. True friendships formed during our formative years stay with us forever. We may meet many people in the journey of our life, but the bonds that are forged in our early years stay with us throughout our life.

Though they haven't met for several years, once their reunion takes place at a ranch, it's almost like they never went. It's like they were there with each other forever, throughout life's difficulties and challenges, giving each other strength and solace. They caught up exactly from where they left.

Steel often weaves magical and vivid tales that beautifully capture the essence of friendship through the challenges they face in life.

17. Life is Cycle of Joys and Sorrows

Steel's stories often highlight life's cycles of joys and sorrows, of cold winters turning into fuzzy summers, and counting the little blessings in life despite the tragedies. With every new person and every new situation we encounter, there's renewed hope.

Once we're done with the crisis, there's reason to smile. Once the darkness of the night gets over, we experience the brightness of daylight. Once tragedy and grief get end, there's a ray of sunshine waiting for us. It just reinforces the saying that, "you've got to put up with the rain if you want to experience the beauty of the rainbow." Every tragedy comes with a silver lining if we have the patience and perseverance to recognize it, and be prepared to move ahead with a new beginning in life.

In The House on Hope Street, Liz and Jack Sutherland lead a perfect life with everything going wonderfully for them, including a happy family home they built together on Hope Street. One Christmas morning, everything falls apart when an errand ends in a tragedy. However, there are the tiny little blessings such as her children that give Liz hope of new beginnings. The next Christmas brings with it the opportunity to start a new life after a year of sorrowful changes and mourning.

Danielle Steel nicely depicts the changing seasons of human emotions and how nothing, even the toughest tragedies are not forever. There are good times ahead. One just has to have the faith to hold on to the silver lining that brings with a promise for a better tomorrow. Her tales are intricate and woven with equally powerful emotions of despair and hope. The protagonists often find themselves in heart-wrenching situations that will make you cry buckets, but in the end- they emerge triumphant. They hold on to their loved ones and a sliver of hope to rise above all the challenges that threaten their happiness.

18. Friendships are the Basis of Love

Several stories of Danielle Steel's involve two diverse people from different backgrounds but similar life situations start as great friends, which subsequently blossoms into a torrid romance. Even the married folks who share a wonderful relationship are shown as being great friends first before being great partners and parents. Friendships form the basis of romantic relationships in Steel's novels. They are the core on which solid romantic alliances are forged.

The protagonists often meet in the unlikeliest situations and develop a deep friendship and mutual respect that over a period of time grows into love. They learn to share their most intimate secrets, joys, sorrows and dreams. There's a deep connect and understanding of the other's inner most personality layers, which is characteristically true of our closest friends and soul mates. Danielle Steel's stories reinforce the power of friendship in strengthening bonds of love.

19. The Concept of Soul mates is Real

Through innumerable stories, Danielle Steel never fails to hint at the concept of soul mates. Though rationalists may scoff at the idea of soul mates for life, she deftly weaves her tales around the power of soul mates and connected hearts. Steel's protagonists are people, who through a series of challenging and fulfilling events discover their soul mates and believe in the power of a karmic connection. The idea that someone somewhere is truly made for you, and is your soul mate forever constantly makes its way into her stories. Through life's adventures and journey, we almost always find that one person who is meant to be our companion across lifetimes. The instant karmic connect, the need to want to talk to the person, the need to spend your entire life with that person – all stems from a greater soulful and spiritual connection that is beyond the purview of a rationalist view of relationships. This is where not mere bodies or minds, but souls entwine.

Michael Hillyard and Nancy McAllister from The Promise illustrate the idea of soul mates beautifully. They are thrown apart following a terrible accident that is destined to change the course of their life forever. Each lives a new life, in a new city after the accident, having left their past behind. But can soul mates be really left behind? Nothing is strong enough to keep them apart since they've made a vow to be with each other forever. However much the forces work to keep soul mates apart, the higher connection always finds a way to manifest.

20. True Love Doesn't Die With Death

Many of Danielle Steel's gripping stories are about protagonists who are left to deal with sudden storms in their lives after years of blissful existence. This includes death, war, destruction, widowhood and other tragedies. However, one idea that strongly stands out among all the devastation is that love doesn't die with the death of a loved one.

Bernie from Fine Things is coming to terms with a life without his wife and the prospect of raising his kids alone. However, the love, hope and healing never stop. The memories don't fade. The love doesn't go away.

Even is her autobiographical account of her son Nick's death in His Bright Light, Danielle Steel talks about creating a loving legacy despite the devastating illness that gripped her son during his lifetime. It presents to us the joy of hope, living, healing, caring and understanding. It underlines the notion that our loved ones, no matter how far they go, always remain strongly etched in our hearts. The joy they've give us, the memories we have of them, the love they leave behind is always there for us to feel when they aren't physically present with us.

21. Our Upbringing Shapes Our Personalities

In a classic nature versus nurture debate, Danielle Steel has reinforced the importance that nurture has on our life and upbringing. For instance, Kaleidoscope talks about the life of three sisters who are orphaned and separated as kids due to tragic circumstances. The book traces their journey of life, and discovers that though they all belong to the same bloodline; they've turned up drastically different in life, based on their environment and circumstances.

Though our genes remain the same, the environment we grow up in influences, to a large extent, our personalities, attitude, behavior, lifestyle, beliefs, culture and several other factors.

Megan, Alexandra and Hilary are three sisters who grow up in different circumstances and backgrounds, following the tragedy in their lives. While Megan is adopted by a comfortably placed family and goes on to become a doctor in Appalachia, Alexandra is raised in the lap of opulence and goes on to marry a very powerful man from a renowned family. Hilary, on the other hand, builds a strong career and has a nonexistent personal life.

The book is a classic ode to the nurture school of thought that reiterates the fact that even siblings sharing the same biological gene pool can also turn out to be dramatically different if they are raised in different environments.

22. Big Business Empires can be Created if You Have the Passion and Spirit

The idea is beautifully revealed in Danielle Steel's Jewels. It is set in the aftermath of World War I, when the Whitfields purchase jewels as a goodwill gesture from impoverished survivors. The protagonist and matriarch, Sarah, has a good eye for aesthetics. Their collection soon grows into a full-fledged jewelry store in Paris. A fine taste in jewelry, and a passion for all things beautiful and rare helps Sarah forge a strong family enterprise that thrives through decades.

Jewels deftly illustrates the idea that if you are truly passionate about something and have the knack of seizing the right opportunity, there's nothing that can stop you from converting your passion into a powerful money making enterprise.

23. Love is an Unpredictable Adventure

Danielle Steel does the love is a rather unpredictable adventure premise brilliantly. She makes her characters fall in love in the unlikeliest of ways sometimes, when the reader is least expecting it.

Toxic Bachelors traces the heady life of three charming and single men, who are averse to the idea of commitment for different reasons. Charlie Harrington, Gray Hawk and Adam Weiss are all grappling with commitment issues that are stopping them from experiencing fulfilling relationships. They have sort of perfected the art of unrealistic expectations, fears and the knack of subjecting themselves to troubled relationships.

On a yacht holiday, they're forced to confront a major truth in each of their lives, and come to terms with their inner most fears about relationships. They have to heal the wounds of the past and deal with women who are all set to fight their existing terrors. The trio of Toxic Bachelors go on to discover how love can be one of the most unpredictable journeys, and how despite being filled with uncertainty and complexity can give us the deepest joys and surprises in life.

24. Strong Friendships Can be Forged in the Face of Tragedies

Danielle Steel knows how to tug at the heartstrings of her readers by helping her protagonists discover new bonds in the face of tragedy. She tells stories of powerful friendships built as a result of tragedy and in the quest for healing. She writes about how true friendship and love can help us heal after life's greatest challenges.

Safe Harbor is all about the power of strong friendships developed during the lowest phases of our life and how they can transform our life forever. It tells the story of 11-year old Pip McKanzie who discovers Matt's steady patience and gentle guidance endearing in the midst of all the challenges. Living in the shadow of her mother, Ophelia's depression, the new companion (fighting his own battles) comes as a ray of hope in the darkness of their lives. We may not recognize it when it happens, but strong friendships forged during the leanest periods of our lives have the ability to transform our existence.

25. Sometimes You Have to Make the Tough Decision of Letting Go of People Who Betray Your Trust

Sometimes, even though its seemingly tough, we have to let go off the toxic people in our life who betray the precious trust we place in them. This is even more painful when people betraying your trust are the ones you thought were the closest to you.

Betray portrays this rather candidly. At the heart of the story, is Talle, a renowned director who finds herself in the midst of betrayal at the hands of the very people she trusts the most. When she discovers the bitter truth, Talle has to gather herself and reinvent her life. She has to make tough decisions despite her emotions to weed out the toxic elements that don't deserve a place in her life. It may require courage and the ability to move out of our comfort zone. It may need you to challenge existing power equations. It may need you to start life afresh with all its challenges and inconveniences, but these decisions are important if you want to take control of your life away from people who don't always have your best interests in mind.

25 OTHER QUICK LESSONS FROM DANIELLE STEEL'S NOVELS

1. We Can Be Winners Despite All the Tragedies That Hold Us Back

Danielle Steel spins a magical tale of love, survival, hope, triumph and impossible victories after unimaginable tragedies in Winners. It shows us nothing can defeat us until we ourselves accept defeat from life.

2. Not Everything is as it Appears to be at First Instance

Don't judge a book by its cover. Don't take everything at face value. In Prodigal Son, though Peter comes across as the selfish son and Michael as the ideal son out of a set of fraternal twins, it's not really what it seems in the beginning as the story progresses.

3. New People Can Help Us Explore Newer Facets About Ourselves

Danielle Steel is an ace at exploring complex relationships and how it can transform us. In Country, she explores how a sudden connection with someone can help us discover multiple layers in ourselves which we didn't even know existed. Stephanie Adams is happy playing mother and wife to the hilt until tragedy strikes and she's left to fend for herself and her children. A chance encounter helps us rediscover herself and give herself a new life that she hadn't ever thought was possible earlier.

4. Life's Challenges Can be Handled Better if You Have Someone By Your Side

Marshall Everett and Ariana Gregory from Steel's Undercover help explore this premise wonderfully in the backdrop of the secret services and international undercover agents. They face a series of challenges, which become relatively conquerable once they stop facing it alone.

5. Sometimes those Maintaining the Outwardly Appearance of a Perfect Life Are the Ones Fighting the Toughest Battles

In a Perfect Life, Blaise McCarthy is a single mother to Salima, blinded as a result of Type 1 diabetes in her childhood. It shows us how when all the facades start crumbling around us, we cannot escape the truth. We have to face the truth to come out of the shadows of illusion and start life afresh.

6. Follow Your Destiny

In Wanderlust, Danielle Steel's protagonist Audrey Driscoll throws caution to winds and breaks traditional stereotypes to follow her wanderlust dreams. Though her path is strewn with danger, conflict, challenges and shocking truths, she is following her destiny by shaking off the complacency to redefine her future. Audrey plunges into the world of conflict and historic events from the shackles of her traditional role to fulfill her destiny.

7.   Never Look Back In Regret

Steel's stories are replete with strong protagonists that quickly learn from the setbacks in their lives and relationships to realize that people who betray our trust and don't value our presence are not worthy of sharing our life's journey. They go on to create wonderful lives for themselves without looking at the past with a sense of regret. Summer's End is about Deanne who after years of wedded bliss follows her heart and finds true love in another man without any regret when she discovers her husband's philandering ways.

8.   The Only Person You Can Rely On is Yourself

Steel never forgets to reinstate the fact that sometimes the only person you can rely on to fight the biggest challenges in life is yourself. There may be other people around you but nothing can be more powerful than the strength within you. Her characters often overcome life's most spirited battles with their spirit intact. Steel often drives home the point on not relying on anyone but yourself to come out unscathed from the wounds life gives you.

9.   You Have To Move On to Fulfill Your Dreams

In Wanderlust and The Apartment both, Danielle Steel talks about moving away from places where your dreams begin to places where you need to go to fulfill them. Life can present us with plenty of unexpected opportunities and chances that we need to keep ourselves open to. Though the places where we begin always hold a special place in our hearts, when the time comes, we have to move away.

10. Nature is a Powerful Force

In Rushing Waters, and several other stories, Danielle Steel shows us how natural disasters can change our lives in an instant. The story is set amidst the backdrop of a natural disaster of huge proportions. It reveals the resilience, hope, courage, and the chance of a new life that natural catastrophes bring with them. It also shows us how nature can be the biggest equalizer of all, and irrespective of who or what you are, it is a fierce and powerful force that can destroy everything.

11. Life Can Change in An Instant

Danielle Steel's novels are always replete with twists and turns that can change a character's life in an instant. She always focuses on life as a rollercoaster ride with its constant ups and downs. Many of her stories are about people living perfectly happy and content lives until a disaster changes everything in an instant. We often take for granted our good times and live under the illusion that they will last forever. Sometimes this illusion is cruelly shattered.

12. The Power of a Sibling's Love Can Be Very Strong

Mirror Image is the story of a set of identical twins, Victoria and Olivia, set amidst a war backdrop. It reveals the magic and eternal power of a sibling's love and how it can help us turn into strong individuals. Siblings are always a joy, and some of our most heart-warming and fun childhood moments are spent in the company of our siblings, who help us build our personalities. The bond and healing power of a sibling's love can be second to none.

13. We Have to Make Tough Choices in Our Pursuit for Freedom

Sometimes we have to move out of our comfort zones to

chase the freedom we crave. Though life may seem cushy and familiar, our quest for freedom may take us to unknown terrors only to rediscover our courage and creativity. Danielle Steel has explored this premise wonderfully in Bittersweet.

14. Sometimes All We Require is a Leap of Faith

In Leap of Faith, Danielle Steel weaves a story about how nothing is what it looks like for the protagonists who has been pulled into a destination far away from her home. There's lies and deceit, until Marie-Ange Hawkins decides to take the ultimate leap pf faith to protect herself and her dear ones.

15. Despair Can be Turned Into Freedom and Loss Into Joy

Many of Steel's stories such as Dating Game are about people who beautifully transform the tragedies of their life into a new freedom and joy. The protagonist of Dating Game, Paris Armstrong, is left devastated when her husband of several years drops her like a hot for a younger woman. Gradually however, with a set of loving friends, she discovers her joy and freedom in what earlier seemed like a tragedy.

16. Some Things Can Never Change When We're With Old Friends

Read Danielle Steel's The Ranch to understand this better. It is a story about three friends who come together after several years for a reunion of sorts. Though their lives have changed, they have their own challenges and secrets, and are at different positions in life, some things that brought them together as friends in their college don't change.

17. The Voices of Loved Ones We've Lost Always Echo in Our Heart

Echoes by Danielle Steel beautifully depicts how the voice of our loved ones never dies but is always guiding us and giving us strength from within. Whether it is our grandparents, parents, spouses, children or friends, their spirit is always around to guide us through the challenges of life. Their loving strength urges us to overcome the toughest situations in life.

18. The Strength, Courage and Determination of a Woman is Remarkably High

The female protagonists of Danielle Steel's novels are extremely courageous, determined and braved. They face innumerable hardships such as war, death, disease, relationship challenges and more only to emerge victorious in the face of challenges. A woman has unlimited reserves of courage and perseverance, and can put up a spirited fight in the toughest situations life throws at her.

19. The World of Glamour is Not Really as Perfect as It Looks

Danielle Steel's Secrets, set in New York and Los Angeles, in the perfect world of a television series talks about how everything is not like it seems in the glamour industry. The perfection can be a mere illusion and there can be plenty of heartache, challenges and secrets underlying the world of performers/entertainers.

20. You Can Have it All

Life is not always about making choices. It doesn't always have to be a choice between love or career, between motherhood or work, between following your passion or simply being at peace with yourself. You can have it all if you want. Tana Roberts, the protagonist of Full Circle discovers that life can actually come a full circle, and she can have it all without sacrificing one for the other.

21. Keepsakes Can Help Us Derive Strength

Danielle Steel's The Ring is about how Arina von Gotthard draws strength from the memory of her dead mother through a ring given to her by her father after the death of her mother. Though on an unfamiliar terrain where her she's battling between a lost past and an uncertain future, the ring is the only piece of hope she clings on to. Sometimes, the mementos our loves ones leave behind for us are the only things that give us the power and hope of their presence.

22. Miracles Can be Experienced in the Smallest Ways in Everyday Life

Miracles are not always huge events in our lives that come with attached labels of miracles. They can be experienced in the smallest and most subtle ways in our daily life. They can touch our lives in little joyous ways to make us laugh, hope, live, learn and appreciate life. Danielle Steel's Miracle explains this rather poignantly.

23. Fate is a Powerful and Irresistible Force

We can have the fanciest ideas for our lives and plan it to perfection, but destiny may have other plans in store for us. Nothing is above fate as a powerful and irresistible force that shapes our life. It is a brilliant equalizer, and even the most formidable and powerful people realize that they are mere puppets in the hands of fate. Danielle Steel's Until the End of Time depicts the idea of love and fate beautifully.

24. Fear of Losing Grip and Getting Hurt Can Often Stop

Us From Getting True Love – Danielle Steel's First Sight is a complex and gripping story that is filled with several love and life lessons. When two determined people from diverse backgrounds come together, the fear of getting hurt and letting go of control often stops us from enjoying fulfilling relationships. We fiercely guard our freedom, don't hand over control of our lives easily, and don't make ourselves vulnerable. We often see relationships as something that is hurting and controlling, which it may not be. At times, it's alright to bare ourselves to the beauty of real love without the fear of getting hurt. We need to be brave enough to face our fears and give love a chance when it comes knocking on our doorstep.

25. What Price Are You Willing to Pay For Your Success?

While it is good to go all out to make your dreams come true, what price does one pay to be highly successful? Is success the only thing in life? Should it be at the cost of our loves ones, values and innumerable sacrifices? Where does one stop when it comes to paying a price for our success? Steel's Power Play is a brilliant story of two CEOs and how they tackle their inner demons and the price they ultimately pay for the high profile lives they lead. Everything, even success comes at a price, and we must decide whether we want to pay that price to be successful.

5 CONCLUSION

In conclusion we can see that the work of Danielle Steel speaks to our hopes and dreams. It recognizes that there is something more to life than struggle or seeking power though that is somehow important too. She speaks to and from our hearts and minds and probably more profoundly, when we read Danielle Steel's work we recognize our longing for connection and love for ourselves and each other and world. Danielle Steel's writings speak from some part of the Soul longing for it's Self which is played out through the longing of that one True Love, the Everlasting Love.

The End

ABOUT THE AUTHOR

Cleopatra Mark lives in Washington State among her many rescue dogs and piles of exotic fabrics which she cuts into small shapes and turns into beautiful quilts. They are both works of art and warm blankets. She grew up reading the Little House on the Prairie series by Laura Ingalls Wilder as a young girl but turned to Danielle Steel when she was in college while listening to Motown Music in Detroit back in the days when Detroit was DETROIT.

Made in United States
Orlando, FL
06 February 2022

14491384R00033